Ancient Greece

BY WILLIAM CAPER

Table of Contents

Introduction

You may not know it, but ancient Greece is a big part of your life. Do you read stories about people like King Midas? He is from Greece. Do you watch the Olympics? They were started by the ancient Greeks. You live in a **democracy**. This type of government began with the ancient Greeks.

Have you ever looked something up in an *encyclopedia*? Have you looked through a *microscope*?

Do you talk on the *telephone* or watch television? The names of all these things come from Greek words.

We know a lot about the ancient Greeks because we can read the works of their writers. And we are discovering more about the ancient Greek world that started 3,000 years ago. **Archaeologists** continue to dig up the **ruins**, or remains, of Greek cities, **temples**, and palaces.

In this book you will learn about the history and **culture** of ancient Greece. As you read, think about what it was like to live there. Also, think about all the ways the ancient Greeks still affect us today.

Get ready to travel back a few thousand years, to a distant land and a far-away time. Explore the world of ancient Greece.

Statues of maidens, or Caryatids, stand as columns on the south side of the Acropolis.

▲ south side of the Acropolis

The Mycenaean Culture:

2000 B.C.–1200 B.C.

Macedonia

Thessaly

Ionian Sea

Attica

Athens

Mycenae

Peloponnese

Area of Detail

G reek **civilization** began around 2000 B.C. At that time, people from the north settled in Greece and started small towns. One of the towns in the south, Mycenae (my-SEE-nee), became large and powerful. The culture that grew up in Greece during this time is called the Mycenaean (my-seh-NEE-en) culture.

The Mycenaean people were warriors and traders. They traded things like olive oil, animal skins, wine, and pottery with people in Egypt and on the island of Crete (KREET). The people on Crete were called Minoans (mih-NOH-ins). The Mycenaeans used parts of Minoan culture. They used the Minoan system of writing. They also used some styles of Minoan **architecture** in their buildings.

THE MINOTAUR

The Minotaur was a creature from a Greek myth. According to the myth, the Minotaur had the head and tail of a bull, and the body of a man. It terrorized the people of Crete. The king of Crete built a huge labyrinth and locked the Minotaur inside. A labyrinth has many connecting passageways, so it is easy to get lost inside. A man named Theseus (THEE-see-us) unwound a ball of thread as he found his way through the labyrinth. He killed the Minotaur. Then he followed the thread out of the labyrinth.

Black Sea

Sea of Marmara

Hellespont

Asia Minor

Aegean Sea

Sea of Crete

Rhodes

SCALE OF MILES

0   50   100

Crete

▲ The Minoans built beautiful palaces. The biggest was the Palace of Minos.

The Mycenaeans were very war-like. They built their cities with thick walls around them to keep out invaders. They conquered the Minoans. They also waged war against other countries around the Aegean (ih-JEEW-ihn) Sea. The Mycenaeans fought their most famous war when they attacked the city of Troy. This war is called the Trojan War.

About 1200 B.C., the Mycenaean civilization fell apart. Its main cities were destroyed. **Historians**, people who study history, do not know what happened. They do not know why Mycenaean culture came to an end.

THE TROJAN HORSE

According to legend, the Greeks won the Trojan War with a clever plan. When they sailed away, they left behind a large wooden horse. The horse was hollow. Greek soldiers were hiding inside. That night, as the Trojans slept, the Greeks sneaked out of the horse and captured the city.

After the collapse of Mycenae, Greece began a time called the Dark Age. During the Dark Age, the Greeks forgot about writing. They kept track of history by singing songs and saying poems about past events.

After 800 B.C., the Greeks began to write again. A poet named Homer wrote down two poems about the Trojan War. Homer wrote these stories as **epics**, or long poems that tell a story. Homer's epics are still read today.

THEY MADE A DIFFERENCE

It is believed that Homer wrote his famous epics between 800 and 700 B.C. The Iliad is about the Trojan War. The Odyssey describes the adventures of the Greek hero Odysseus (oh-DIH-see-us) after the war. In ancient Greece, children studied these poems in school. Today, people still learn about ancient Greece by reading The Iliad and The Odyssey.

The Growth of the City-States: 800 B.C.-480 B.C.

During the Dark Age, the Greeks left their cities and lived in small tribes. Slowly, these tribes grew larger and began trading with one another. They began to share things and work together against enemies. As more and more people came together, small cities began to grow.

▲ the Acropolis today

To protect their cities, the Greeks built defenses on a hill. These defenses were called an **acropolis** (uh-CROP-uh-lihs). Part of the Acropolis was a palace. The palace was the king's home, and a place of safety. Important temples were also built on the Acropolis. The Acropolis was the military and religious center of the ancient Greek city.

There were two other important places in a city. One was the **agora** (AG-uhr-uh). The other was the **gymnasium** (jim-NAY-zee-um). The agora was an open area in the middle of the city. It was a market and a place for Greeks to meet and talk. Gymnasiums were schools where boys received physical and military training.

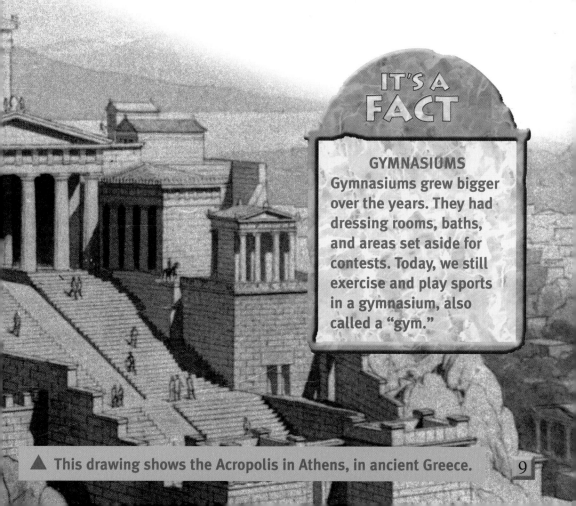

IT'S A FACT

GYMNASIUMS
Gymnasiums grew bigger over the years. They had dressing rooms, baths, and areas set aside for contests. Today, we still exercise and play sports in a gymnasium, also called a "gym."

▲ **This drawing shows the Acropolis in Athens, in ancient Greece.**

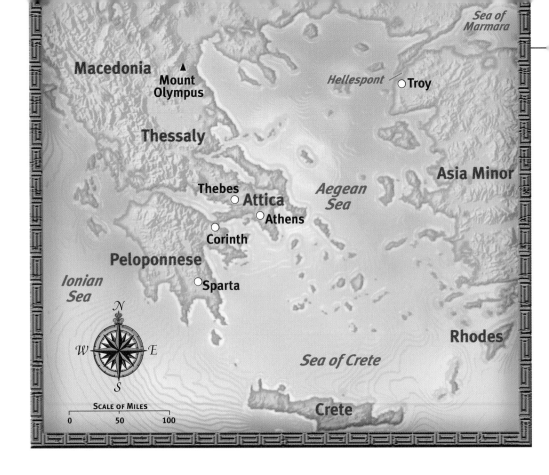

Greek cities were not cities the way we think of them today. They were more like separate countries. Each city ruled the land around it. It had its own customs and government. The word for city was *polis* (PAH-lihs), or city-state. Our word "political" comes from this Greek word. The most important **city-states** were Athens, Sparta, Thebes (THEEBS), and Corinth (KOR-inth).

City-states had two groups of people—**citizens** and noncitizens. Citizens were from families who had always lived in the city. Only citizens could own land and take part in the government. Noncitizens were people from other city-states and other countries. Women and slaves were also noncitizens.

The Beginning of Democracy

At first, kings ruled the city-states. By about 750 B.C., many kings had been overthrown by **nobles**, or people of high rank.

In some city-states, a new form of government was beginning. This new form of government was democracy. The word *democracy* means rule by the people. These early democracies were run by the free male citizens. Women, slaves, and other noncitizens had no political rights.

It would be a long time before there would be democracy as we know it. Even so, in ancient Greece more people had a voice in their government than before. The most successful democracy in ancient Greece was Athens.

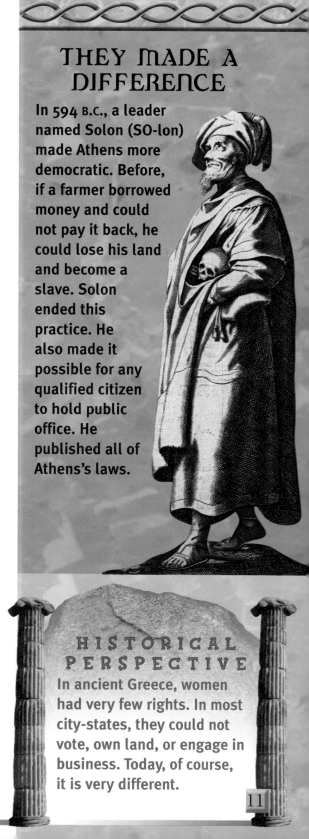

THEY MADE A DIFFERENCE

In 594 B.C., a leader named Solon (SO-lon) made Athens more democratic. Before, if a farmer borrowed money and could not pay it back, he could lose his land and become a slave. Solon ended this practice. He also made it possible for any qualified citizen to hold public office. He published all of Athens's laws.

HISTORICAL PERSPECTIVE

In ancient Greece, women had very few rights. In most city-states, they could not vote, own land, or engage in business. Today, of course, it is very different.

Persia Invades Greece

In 490 B.C., King Darius of Persia sent an army and a fleet of ships to conquer Athens. (Persia was a kingdom to the east of Greece.) The Greeks and the Persians came face to face in Marathon. This city was about 26 miles (42 kilometers) northeast of Athens. There were more Persians than Greeks. But the Greeks were able to surround and defeat the Persian army.

The Persians still had their ships, and they sailed to attack Athens. The leader of the Greek army sent a messenger to Athens to warn the city of the coming attack. When the Persian ships arrived at Athens, the Greeks were ready. The Persians turned around and sailed back to their home.

The messenger sent to Athens after the battle at Marathon was Pheidippides (fy-DIP-ih-deez). He ran the whole way, 26 miles, in about three hours. But he was exhausted, and after he delivered his message he fell down and died. Today, the word *marathon* refers to a foot race of 26 miles 385 yards (about 42.2 kilometers).

SOLVE THIS

1. According to some accounts, the Persians outnumbered the Greeks at Marathon 4 to 1. If the Greeks had 12,000 men, how many men did the Persians have?

The Persians still wanted to conquer the Greeks. In 480 B.C., Darius's son, King Xerxes (ZERK-seez), sent a huge army and fleet to invade Greece. Many of the Greek city-states joined together to fight the Persians. The Persians defeated a Greek army north of Athens.

Then the Perisans went on to Athens. But the Greek navy was waiting for them there. The Greek navy sank about half the Persian fleet. The Greeks defeated the rest of the Persian soldiers in 479 B.C.

▲ Greeks attacking Persian ships during the battle of Marathon

Athens and Sparta

In the war with Persia, the Greek city-states worked together and won a great victory. Sparta led the Greeks on land. Athens led the Greeks at sea. Athens now had the most powerful fleet in the Aegean Sea. Some city-states turned to Athens for protection. Athens became very powerful. Some city-states turned to Sparta for protection. That made Sparta stronger.

ATHENS

In Athens, boys studied reading, writing, and mathematics. They trained to become soldiers. But to Athenians, there was more to life than being a soldier. Students also learned to give public speeches and play musical instruments.

Athenian women did not have the same freedom as women in Sparta. Most young women received no education. Their mothers taught them skills like cooking, making clothing, and taking care of babies.

Athens and Sparta were very different. Each had its own ideas and customs about men, women, education, and how to live. As Athens and Sparta grew in power, they stopped trusting each other. Each city-state thought it was the strongest. This led to trouble between the city-states.

SPARTA

In Sparta, life centered around the army. When a Spartan boy reached the age of seven, he was sent to military and athletic school. After thirteen years of training, he became a soldier. For a Spartan, the greatest honor was to die defending his city in battle.

Spartan women had much more freedom than women in other city-states. As girls, they took part in athletic activities. As women, they could be in business.

The Golden Age of Ancient Greece:
480 B.C.-431 B.C.

T he term *Golden Age* refers to a time when a culture or nation is at its greatest. The Golden Age in Athens was during the mid-400s B.C.

Theater

During the Golden Age, theater—especially tragedy—became very important. A tragedy is a serious play. Greek tragedies were usually about a person who faced a very difficult decision. Tragedies had unhappy endings.

Tragedies were part of a big festival held each year. The festival lasted for many days. Prizes were given for the best plays and the best acting. Comedies, or funny plays, were also performed. In Athens, there was an outdoor theater that had room for about 14,000 people.

Greek plays are still performed today. Even though they were written thousands of years ago, many of the ideas in these plays are still important.

These are the ruins of the theater in the ancient

IT'S A FACT

In ancient Greek theaters, actors and singers wore masks that showed happiness and sadness. Today, these masks have come to stand for tragedy and comedy.

History

Another new kind of writing was writing about history. A man named Herodotus (hih-RAH-dih-tus) traveled all around the Mediterranean Sea. He studied the peoples who lived there and their pasts. He wrote about the things he learned.

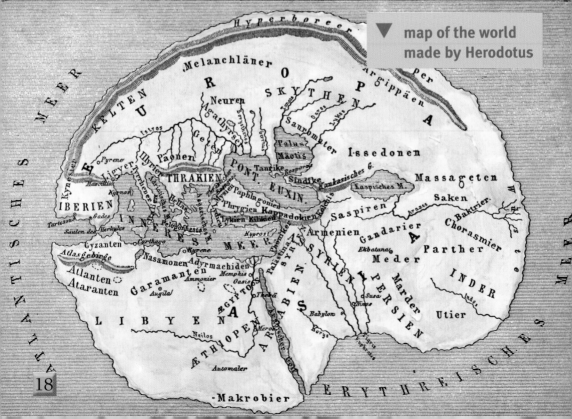

▼ map of the world made by Herodotus

Philosophy

Philosophy (fih-LAS-uh-fee) began in ancient Greece. The word comes from two Greek words meaning "love of wisdom." One of the most important Greek philosophers was Socrates (SAH-kruh-teez). He explored a subject by asking people questions. These questions showed the weaknesses in someone's ideas.

THEY MADE A DIFFERENCE

Socrates taught by constantly asking questions. For example, he might ask, "What is truth?" Socrates did not answer his questions. But as other people tried to answer, he kept asking more questions. It became clear that people did not really know what they thought they did.

▲ 19th-century engraving of Socrates teaching

Architecture

Greek architects were also busy at work. They built many temples. Temples usually had columns around an inner room. The most famous temple was the Parthenon (PAR-thuh-non) in Athens. The Parthenon was on the Acropolis.

Sculpture

Greek sculptors created beautiful statues. They carved statues of gods, goddesses, and people. The statue of Zeus at Olympia was one of the Seven Wonders of the Ancient World.

✓ POINT

THINK ABOUT IT

In what ways was the world of the ancient Greeks similar to our world today? In what ways was the ancient Greek world different from our world today?

Science

One Greek scientist said that everything was made of tiny bits of material called atoms. Hippocrates (hih-PAH-krih-teez) taught that diseases have natural causes. He said that the body can heal itself. These were bold ideas that helped people think about the world in new and different ways.

SOLVE THIS

2. The Parthenon is about 18 meters high. If one meter equals about 3.3 feet, how high is the Parthenon in feet?

21

GODS AND GODDESSES OF THE ANCIENT GREEKS

The ancient Greeks believed in many gods and goddesses. Each city-state gave special respect to at least one god or goddess. The Greeks believed that their gods and goddesses were very powerful. They also believed the gods were immortal, which means "able to live forever."

Here are some of the gods and goddess of the ancient Greeks:

Zeus	Ruler of the gods
Poseidon	God of the sea
Hades	God of the underworld, ruler of the dead
Hera	Wife of Zeus
Ares	God of war
Athena	Goddess of wisdom
Apollo	God of music, light, and truth He drove the sun across the sky each day.
Aphrodite	Goddess of love
Hermes	Messenger of the gods

Athena

Apollo

▲ Olympic competition in ancient Greece

The Olympic Games

The first known Olympic Games were held in 776 B.C. at Olympia in western Greece. After that, they were held every four years. In the first thirteen games, there was only one event—a running race of 192 meters (210 yards). Over the years, other events were added such as wrestling, boxing, chariot racing, and horse racing. The Olympic Games were so important to the ancient Greeks that they even stopped wars for them. In A.D. 393, a Roman emperor ended the games. The modern Olympic Games began in 1896.

The Fall of Ancient Greece

431 B.C.–338 B.C.

▲ Battle of Thermopylae

B y working together, the Greeks were able to defeat the Persians. But the Greeks were not able to live in peace with one another for very long. Athens and Sparta went to war with each other in 431 B.C. This war is known as the Peloponnesian (peh-leh-puh-NEE-zhen) War.

For many years the war went back and forth. Both sides won victories. Then things went in favor of Sparta. By this time, Sparta was friends with the Persians! In 404 B.C., Athens finally gave up. The Spartans destroyed the walls of the city. They said that Athens could no longer have a navy. They also ended Athens' democracy. The Golden Age of Greece was over. Now Sparta was the most powerful city-state in Greece.

But warfare continued. This made the city-states weaker. At the same time, a country close to Greece was growing stronger.

SOLVE THIS

3. The Golden Age of Greece lasted from 480 B.C. to 431 B.C. How many years is this?

Another Invasion

Macedonia (ma-sih-DOH-nee-uh) was a country to the north of Greece. In 353 B.C., Philip II, king of Macedonia, invaded Greece. In 338 B.C., Macedonia defeated the Greeks. Greece was now ruled by Macedonia.

▲ Macedonian soldiers fought in groups like this one. Their long spears allowed them to strike at their enemy from as far away as twenty feet.

Alexander the Great

Philip's next plan was to lead a Macedonian and Greek army against Persia, but he was killed. His son, Alexander, became ruler of Macedonia. Alexander admired the Greeks. He helped spread Greek culture to Egypt and the Near East.

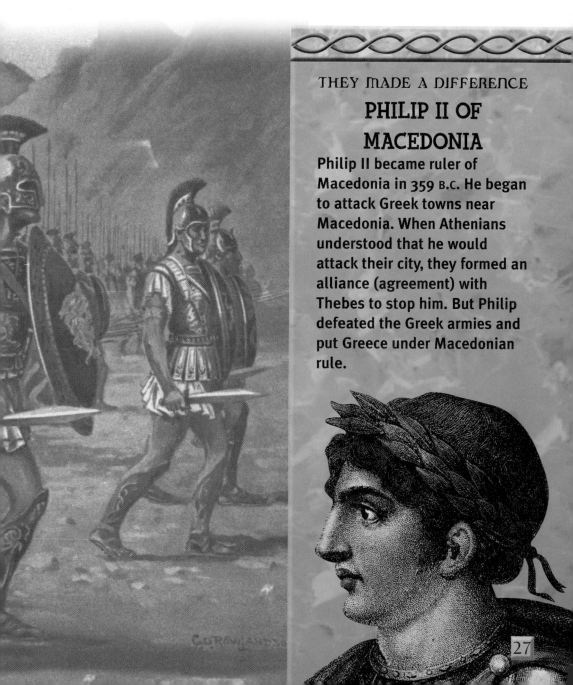

THEY MADE A DIFFERENCE

PHILIP II OF MACEDONIA

Philip II became ruler of Macedonia in 359 B.C. He began to attack Greek towns near Macedonia. When Athenians understood that he would attack their city, they formed an alliance (agreement) with Thebes to stop him. But Philip defeated the Greek armies and put Greece under Macedonian rule.

27

Conclusion

Today, more than 2,000 years after the Golden Age, it is easy to see how much we owe to the ancient Greeks. Their political leaders gave us democracy. They gave us the ideas of trial by jury and equal treatment under the law. Our modern doctors base their actions on the teachings of Hippocrates. Greek words have given us language we use every day.

Even though we know much about the ancient Greeks, we are still learning more.

☑ POINT

MAKE CONNECTIONS

Many things we do, say, and see today can be traced back to the ancient Greeks. How many can you name?

A Time Line of

About 3000 B.C.	2000–1200 B.C.	776 B.C.
The Minoan culture develops in Crete.	The Mycenaean culture develops in Greece.	The first known Olympic Games take place.

▲ ruins of the Greek city of Delphi

Ancient Greece

490 and 479 B.C.	480–431 B.C.	431–404 B.C.	338 B.C.
The Greeks defeat invading Persian armies.	The Golden Age of Greece. Greek culture reaches its height.	The Peloponnesian War. Sparta defeats Athens.	Philip II of Macedonia conquers Greece.

Our knowledge of them grows each time archaeologists uncover more ruins of this once-mighty civilization. As we look into the past to study their world, the ancient Greeks continue to shape our world.

IT'S GREEK TO US
Here are some common words that come from Greek.

GREEK ROOT	BASIC MEANING	ENGLISH WORD
-dem-	people	democracy
-path-	feeling, suffering	sympathy

GREEK PREFIX	BASIC MEANING	ENGLISH WORD
auto-	self, same	autobiography
bio-	life	biology
geo-	Earth	geography
micro-	small	microscope
therm-	heat	thermometer

GREEK SUFFIX	BASIC MEANING	ENGLISH WORD
-graph	write or draw	autograph
-phone	sound	telephone

Glossary

acropolis (uh-CROP-uh-lihs) a fortified hill in or near an ancient Greek city (page 9)

agora (AG-uhr-uh) an ancient Greek marketplace (page 9)

archaeologist (ar-kee-AHL-uh-jist) a scientist who studies an ancient civilization by looking at its structures and other things its people have left behind (page 2)

architecture (AR-kih-tek-chur) the art and science of building (page 4)

citizen (SIT-ih-zen) a person who lives in a city, town, or country, especially one who is allowed to vote and has other rights there (page 10)

city-state (SIT-ee STAYT) an independent city that has its own government and controls the territory around it (page 10)

civilization (siv-uh-lih-ZAY-shin) the culture developed by a nation or region; an advanced state of development marked by progress in the arts, sciences, and law (page 4)

culture (KUL-chur) the customs, behavior, beliefs, ideas, and arts of a group of people (page 3)

democracy (dih-MOK-reh-see) government by the people (page 2)

epic (EP-ik) a long poem that tells a story, usually about a hero or heroic actions (page 7)

gymnasium (jim-NAY-zee-um) school in Ancient Greece (page 9)

historian (hih-STOR-ee-en) someone who studies or writes about history (page 6)

noble (NO-bil) a person of high birth or rank (page 11)

philosophy (fih-LAHS-uh-fee) investigation of the nature of things and ideas, based on logical reasoning (page 19)

ruins (ROO-inz) what is left after something has been destroyed (page 2)

temple (TEM-puhl) a building where religious services are held (page 2)

Index

SOLVE THIS ANSWERS

1. Page 12   48,000 men
2. Page 21   about 59 feet
3. Page 25   49 years